YOUR KNOWLEDGE HAS VALUE

Arndt Schmidt

Review Essay Refiguring the Archive

GRIN Verlag

Bibliografische Information der Deutschen Nationalbibliothek:

Die Deutsche Bibliothek verzeichnet diese Publikation in der Deutschen National-
bibliografie; detaillierte bibliografische Daten sind im Internet über http://dnb.d-
nb.de/ abrufbar.

Imprint:

Copyright © 2008 GRIN Verlag GmbH
Druck und Bindung: Books on Demand GmbH, Norderstedt Germany
ISBN: 978-3-656-13007-9

This book at GRIN:

http://www.grin.com/en/e-book/189023/review-essay-refiguring-the-archive

Review Essay: "Refiguring the Archive"

Working in archives is indeed "the bread and butter" of the historian. Before they go there for the first time however, hardly any student of history has got a thorough understanding of how archives function and what they represent. Thus, for many it turns out to be a quite intimidating experience, because one can all too easily get lost as one rarely has a definite starting point, let alone a proper map for the first descent. On the other hand, some archives offer guided tours that leave their visitors with a feeling of crossing the thresholds to the halls of the past, imbuing them with a sense of awe before all of that stored evidence.

In my very first semester of studying history at the University of Freiburg, I was taken on such a tour to a department of the German Federal Archives there. Two women took care to render us a lively presentation of their work place. They displayed yellowed historical military maps, let people read out aloud out of tattered war diaries, guided us through a laboratory where people in white coats and safety goggles tried to restore sources that had been damaged by mildew, fire or extinguishing water. The style of their presentation resulted in an image of the archive as a mixture of laboratory and treasure chest. A place where the secrets of the past were locked and waiting for historians to come and reveal them.

Even though the every day work of the historian may turn out to be a bit more sober than this description, the conventional notion of the archive has generally been of a place where *evidence* about past events is being preserved for present and future generations. This implied the assumption that the primary sources uncovered from the archive were to be treated like impartial witnesses, capable of producing objective knowledge about the past, as long as they were interpreted according to historical methodology. Starting from the assumption that such a conventional idea of the archive is very much outdated, the project of *"Refiguring the Archive"* is to *"bring to bear on `archive´ an interrogation similar to that which concepts like `canon´ or `orientalism´ have undergone"* and to *"develop our understanding of the circumstances of the creation of the archival record"*.[1]

In order to understand why the above described notion of archive is outdated in the post-modern world and to see the necessity of interrogating "circumstances of the creation of archival record", it proves helpful to remember some of the origins of such questioning. In 1967, Richard Rorty published an anthology with the title *"The Linguistic Turn. Recent Essays in Philosophical Method"*.[2] Whereas Immanuel Kant had been the first philosopher to formulate the boundaries of human reason, the linguistic turn represented a consequent application of Kant's ideas, since the limits of our thinking are in fact determined by the limits of our language.

Kant does not ask for the essence of being as such anymore, but for the preconditions of experience. These conditions are the pure categories of time, space and reason through which we always already experience reality and which structure our experience before we live it (a priori). Since all experience can be conveyed only by means of language, the linguistic turn implies a fundamental scepticism towards the view of language as a transparent and neutral medium for the communication of reality: No sign, word or concept is identical with the significate that it relates to or that it seeks to define.

---

[1] Hamilton, Carolyn, ed., (2002), Refiguring the Archive, Kluwer Academic Publishers, p. 9.

[2] Rorty, Richard (1967), The Linguistic Turn. Recent Essays in Philosophical Method, Chicago University Press. The book's title seizes upon Gustav Bergmann, who had proclaimed a "linguistic turn" in his essay *"Two Types of Linguistic Philosophy"* from 1952. Cf. Bergmann, Gustav, Two Types of Linguistic Philosophy, in: The Review of Metaphysics, Vol. 5, March 1952, pp. 417-438.

The conventional view of language as neutral medium has therefore been replaced by the notion of language as something that you cannot go beyond: When we speak, we can never fully match any experience – we can only hint at it. Words are always defined by other words and language itself is therefore not more than self-referential system. For history this has meant that we do not ask for historical truths and pure facts anymore. Instead, we turn to the discourse, in which these truths and facts are being articulated. Furthermore, we become aware that as soon as we narrate history, we already interpret it by the way that we structure it.

"Refiguring the Archive" then takes these assumptions for granted and pivots around a number of key questions. What is the conventional idea of an archive? How is this idea being questioned? What functions do archives possess? How should the post-apartheid archive look like? The book itself represents a compilation of essays that are all the product of a conference project that was hosted by the University of the Witwatersrand in 1998 under the same title "Refiguring the Archive". This basically consisted of a series of 13 seminars, but it also involved a number of events that should help to demonstrate a very much extended concept of what might fall under the concept of archive.

Thus, a musical was staged that was produced from archive materials about gay and lesbian township life, an exhibition tried to focus on processes of documentation from an artistic angle, whereas the performance of a dance choreography tried to explore dance as a form of archive in its own right. These artistic influences partly also make themselves felt in the book's original layout that uses intertextuality in order to *"provide a shifting space for multiple voices."*[3]. Three different chapters for example are set parallel to each other on opposite pages, thus undercutting our common sense of structure. This also relates to one of the book's most important claims,

---

[3] Hamilton, p. 14.

namely that there is no ultimate structure of reality that should be taken for granted. Since the first of these respective chapters, a talk given by Jacques Derrida, is being discussed in the other two, the juxtaposition in fact makes all the more sense. Furthermore, generous space is devoted to the presentation of diverse archive materials. The book therefore works against a notion of archives as something dull and dry that is not uncommon even among too many historians.

The assembled essays eventually evolve around three distinct themes. The first section provides a theoretical framework of questioning conventional thinking about archives. The second section becomes more practical in that it shows the making of archives, how power relations are involved in the processes of recording, forgetting and structuring. Examples are drawn from the influence of the state machinery in apartheid South Africa and its "State Archives Service", but also from the hearing practices of the Truth and Reconciliation Commission. The third section strives to broaden our understanding of what falls under the term archive. In this it follows Michel Foucault's understanding of the term, which includes all kinds of institutions like *"libraries, museums, local records and special collections all designed to create a particular vision of society."*[4]

From this also follow two concerns of "Refiguring the Archive". The extension of the boundaries of the term's definition expresses the wish for a broader tendency of inclusion for all of society, since archive always implies *"a conception of what is valuable, and how such value should be transmitted across time."*[5] The other concern is even more fundamental as it assumes an implicit contract between the archivist and society. The book wants to question the tacit nature of that contract by asking what *"archivists undertake to do in return for the enormous power invested in them by*

---

[4] Ibid., p. 15.

[5] Ibid., p. 16.

society?" They are asked to interrogate the epistemological foundations of their work.[6]

Questions of epistemology occupy indeed an important position within "Refiguring the Archive". The main thrust of the book could be put in a nutshell as follows. For most of the time, there was a very straightforward notion of archive. Archives were depositories for collections of mostly written documents, mostly relating to the work of the state and government. They were in fact seen as a kind of treasure chests that could be consulted in order to obtain insights about the past. Since the archives consisted of primary sources which related directly to past events, profound interpretation of these sources would provide clear insights and make reinterpretation and rewriting of history unnecessary. Archives were therefore invested with the authority of authenticity and objectivity.

After the linguistic turn, this view has been challenged. Attention has been drawn to the fact that archives can never establish themselves beyond history. They are constructed by the gathering together of sources in a process that follows specific rules. These in turn establish which sources are worthy to be included and which ones are being excluded and therefore extinguished from historical discourse.

At the same time, this means that archives constitute, according to a phrase by Foucault, "the law of what can be said". Whereas previously historians occupied themselves merely with the content of sources, they now pay attention to the rules that shaped the archival record itself. What set of rules makes archivists include one source – and therefore invest its voice with authority – and omit another one, so that its voice is not being heard and therefore forgotten?

Since they make up the law of what can be said, archives are by no means neutral collections of information. They make certain stories possible to be told while they

---

[6] Ibid., p. 16-17.

leave out others. Moreover, their contents can only be accessed in the first place once they are catalogued according to a specific order. Therefore, a specific sense of coherence is imposed on the archives' contents as well. This coherence however is only an imaginary one, because there are always gaps to be filled which already require an effort of interpretation that precedes the first reading by any historian. Rather than a treasure chest for insights about past events, the archive therefore comes to be seen much more like a mere sliver of the past.

According to the new way of thinking about archives, this would be the case even if one could preserve every single record that was generated. The old view on the archive saw it as reflecting reality in a direct way, almost like a mirror. According to deconstructivist ideas however, any event is held to be unique and in this sense unknowable. Words are never identical with realities. Any recording of an event is therefore only a hint at it.

The record itself is already the outcome of a process of reflection. This process also contains the stains of the people that created it and the archivists that placed items in a specific order. Even the addition of further archive material therefore influences the way in which an individual item can be interpreted. This means that sources can never really reflect the past like a mirror, but only in a fractured and distorted way: at best a sliver of a mirror.

These considerations bring with them some consequences for the way in which the archive system of the apartheid should be transformed. Whereas under apartheid rule archivists claimed to be impartial and objective, they should now acknowledge their role as active shapers of social memory. In the beginning of the discourse on the transformation of archives, it was even expressed that the power of archives should be used in order to promote particular narratives that would be beneficial to the aims of reconciliation and nation building.

This also touches the appraisal of documents and items by archivists. Instead of simply judging the usefulness of an item according to its specific content, the archivists are supposed to identify the key elements of the contextual milieu in which it was produced. In this way, the criteria of content value are being replaced by the provenance of items. Nevertheless, this does not change the fact that the appraiser actively creates archival value.

Another issue is the policy of collecting. Instead of concentrating on the pinnacles of society, archives should take part in the imperative of giving voice to the voiceless. This involves two points. First, according to this objective the public archives in South Africa should not compete with non-public archives for specialist fields, so as to strengthen the position of the latter. Secondly, the public archives are supposed to collect oral sources themselves as well as acquire them from historians who have done research in oral tradition. Apart from these policies, archives are supposed to go beyond the mere providing of services for users and instead actively create users by taking archives to the people. This is especially important because of barriers like illiteracy and huge distances. In short, archives should be turned from elitist institutions into community resources.

"Refiguring the Archive" has got a particular pivot in form of Jacques Derrida and his book "Archive Fever", which seems to have given much impetus for the book's main thrust as well as the seminar series that it resulted from. Two full chapters are devoted to a discussion of his book. Derrida brings psychoanalysis into play with regards to the rules that govern the production, the structuring of archive and the cause to make archives in the first place. He links the cause of archives to the "death drive", calling the wish to store archival material a compulsion. Even Susan Van Zyl concedes at the end of her article, that there may be *"space for a reading of the contribution psychoanalysis can make to questions of the archive that is different from that of Derrida in* Archive Fever, *a reading that might trouble the archive in less mysterious ways".*[7] What psychoanalysis in its own right may have to offer for the deconstruction of archives, apart from this idea of the death drive, remains very much undefined within "Refiguring the Archive". Nevertheless, Verne Harris manages to grasp the relation of Derrida's work to the archive more concretely and thus sums up much of the entire compilation's strength.

Harris sums up four of Derrida's main theses as follows: 1. Past events in their uniqueness are irrecoverable. 2. Archival content may relate to past events, but instead of reflecting them, they always already shape them. 3. Other than speaking for themselves, the archive is always already being interpreted by the scholars who deal with the archival contents. 4. Before scholars start dealing with archive, they are themselves always already marked by their own pre-impressions, which shapes their interpretations.

These points also relate to the death drive that Derrida talks about. The archive always already *"[…] works against itself. This is the 'archive fever' of the book's title".* It is the aporia that is intrinsic to the archive. There can be no memorization without an *"instinct of forgetfulness"* that constitutes the death drive, because without a process of shaping which involves forgetting, there could not be any memorization in the first place.[8] Quoting Derrida, Harris just like Van Zyl, goes on to concede that psychoanalysis does not offer any way out of this aporia. It *"only succeeds in heightening it, for 'it repeats the very thing it resists or which it makes its object.'*[9] Instead of trying to resolve the archive's forgetfulness, one can therefore rather only become conscious of it and acknowledge it. This could at least lead to an inversion of former tendencies of *"closing the archive."* Instead of *"resolving mystery"* once and

---

[7] Ibid., p. 59.

[8] Ibid., p. 65.

[9] Ibid., p. 69.

for all then, *"archival contextualisation reveals the multiple layers of construction in text, and in doing so adds yet another layer. Properly conceived, archival contextualisation, indeed archival endeavour as a whole, should be about the releasing of meanings, the tending of mystery and the disclosing of the archive's openness."[10]*

So to speak, "Refiguring the Archive" is a remarkable book whose strength consists in each essay contributing "another layer" to the disclosure of the constructedness of the archive, to the awareness that the phenomenon of archiving is not about finding the one and only truth about the past, *"but rather to affirm the unknowable (embrace with a ´yes´!, otherness) as the very core of our humanity."[11]*

---

[10] Ibid., p. 71.

[11] Ibid., p. 81.